P9-CMV-448

monday morning®

SUPER CIRCLE TIME

FALL

by Patty Claycomb

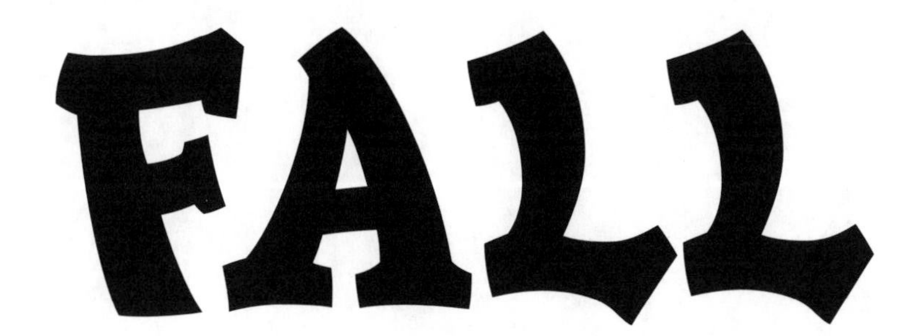

Publisher: Roberta Suid
Production: Little Acorn & Associates, Inc.

SUPER CIRCLE TIME FALL

For a complete catalog, write to the address below:
Monday Morning Books, Inc.
PO Box 1134
Inverness, CA 94937

Call our toll-free number: 1-800-255-6049
E-mail us at: MMBooks@aol.com
Visit our Web site:
http://www.mondaymorningbooks.com

ISBN 1-57612-200-X

Printed in the United States of America
9 8 7 6 5 4 3 2 1

Contents

Introduction

Taking a walk, in fall, is one of the most breathtaking and beautiful experiences you can have. Fall is color! Fall is a sudden breeze that makes leaves dance down streets. Fall is a metamorphosis all its own. It is the ending of warm weather and the approach of crisper air. What happens in between is worth observing and learning about.

If you take a close look at fall, you will see trees changing their appearance and color. You will see changing landscapes. You will see animals searching for food and hoarding it. You will see more clouds and perhaps some rain. You will hear rustling sounds and crunching sounds. You might even grab your collar and give it a tug around your neck. Winter is around the corner!

What else is unique about fall? The moon! The moon appears larger in the sky than any other time during the year. A full autumn moon is spectacular. The moon's glow will light up fields and orchards that will soon be ready to harvest. Pumpkins and squash and apples can be picked and prepared for autumn feasts. Now add some creative thinking. Peel apples in one long curling strip. Eat your apple snake! Make a squash baby. Wrap a large squash in a blanket and pass it around. Give it a name!

And don't forget! This is the season for finding treasures, right beneath your feet. Acorns and seed pods and the birth of pine cones make wonderful art, besides the fun of pure discovery!

Fall is: Colors-Leaves-Sounds-Chills-Jackets-Harvests-Treasures-Discoveries!

Things to talk about:

1. What does the word September mean? Brainstorm! It is the word for the first month of fall. Who can say the word September?
2. Try clapping the word September. Clap slowly on each syllable. You will clap three times. Who wants to clap the word September?
3. How many days does September have? Count to 30. If you have a calendar, point to each number.
4. There is one very special thing that happens in September. What do you think it is? (A new school year starts.)

Materials:

Butcher paper, scissors, tape, a felt marker

Preparation:

Cut a long strip of butcher paper. Tape it on a wall. Print at the top of the paper: "September means:"

Things to do:

September means many things. Begin with the words "September means." Each child, in turn, can finish the sentence. Print each response on the butcher paper. Number the answers. Possible answers are listed below:

September means:

1. a new school
2. making new friends
3. getting a new lunch box
4. getting new shoes
5. learning new things
6. cooler weather
7. trees losing their leaves
8. leaves turning different colors
9. wearing warmer clothes
10. sleeping with a blanket on
11. animals getting ready to hibernate
12. animals eating more food
13. squirrels storing nuts under the ground

More Ideas:

- Tape a strip of paper on the wall. Print the words "In September, I want to:" at the top of the paper. Print each child's response below.

Things to talk about:

1. What are the four seasons? How long is a season? (three months) What season are you in now?
2. What is different about each season? Brainstorm! Possible answers are: The weather is different; Different fruit and flowers grow in each season; You see different kinds of animals in each season; Days are longer in some seasons; Trees look different in the four seasons; The night sky looks different in each season.
3. Who knows the date of their birthday? What season is your birthday in?

Materials: None

Preparation: None

Things to do:

Learn the *Autumn Fall Down Chant*.

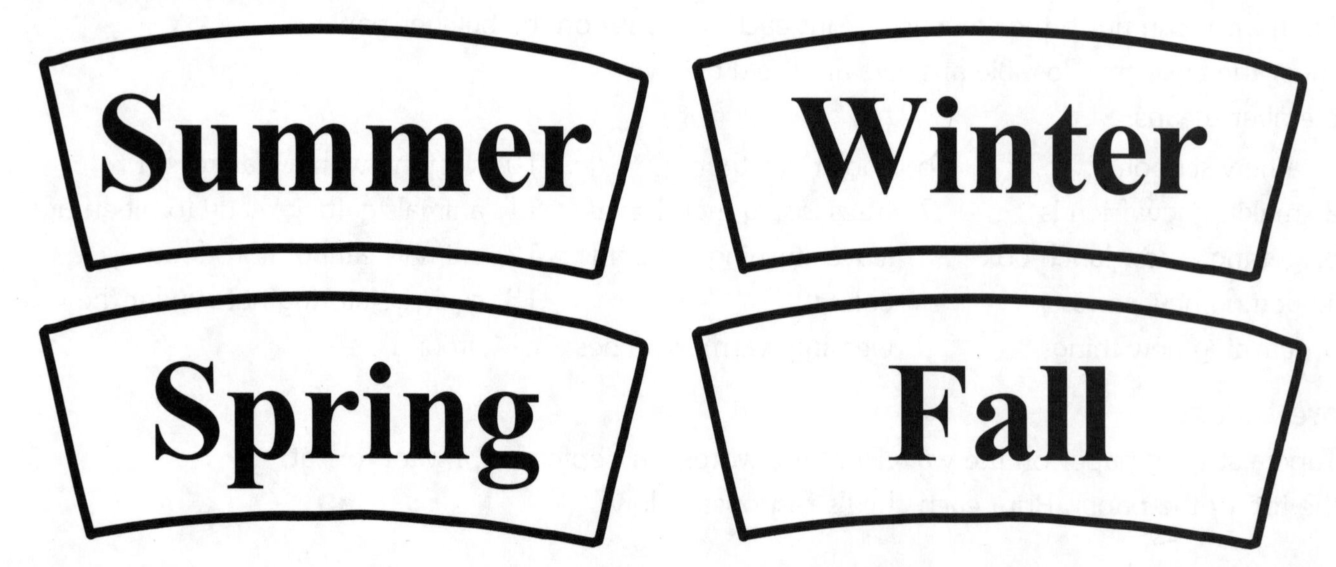

The Fall Down Chant

Seasons come,
And seasons go,
Around and around,
The world we know.
And if I could,
I'd clap my hands,
And stop the spinning,
Of the lands,
To jump right into,
Summer.

I love to feel warm.

Seasons come,
And seasons go,
Around and around,
The world we know.
And if I could,
I'd clap my hands,
And stop the spinning,
Of the lands,
To jump right into,
Fall.

Please fall down.

Seasons come,
And seasons go,
Around and around,
The world we know.
And if I could,
I'd clap my hands,
And stop the spinning,
Of the lands,
To jump right into,
Winter.

I'm hibernating - Shhhhhhhh.

Seasons come,
And seasons go,
Around and around,
The world we know.
And if I could,
I'd clap my hands,
And stop the spinning,
Of the lands,
To jump right into,
Spring.

It's finally getting warmer.

More Ideas:

- Place an empty plastic bottle in the middle of a posterboard. Print the names of the seasons in each corner. Everyone can take turns spinning the bottle. When it lands on a season, say the last line in each verse.

Things to talk about:

1. Sit very still. Close your eyes. Think of a tree. How would it feel if you were a tree? Brainstorm! You might feel tall. You might feel rough and stiff, like a trunk. You might feel cool, bending in a breeze. You might have fun, seeing way above the housetops.
2. Ask questions, such as, "How would it feel to be the wind, or rain, or a large orange pumpkin?"
3. If you could be anything else, besides yourself, what would it be?

Materials: None

Preparation: None

Things to do:

Learn *The Cycle of Life Chant*. This is a chant to be said slowly. This will allow the words and the cycle of life to sink in. Below are suggestions for movement:

- For the first verse, crouch down on the rug. As you say the last two lines, slowly kneel on your knees. When you say the word "out," lift both arms in the air and shout it.
- For the second verse, slowly move into a standing position. Wave your arms around as your branches grow. Wave them around you and over your head.
- For the third verse, when you say the first line, swish both hands back and forth on each seasonal word. For the second line, make fists in the air and open them up. Do this over and over again. For the third line, drop on your knees and thump your hands on the rug for falling pine cones. For the last line, wiggle your fingers on the rug for seeds falling out.
- For the fourth verse, repeat the actions in the first verse.

The Cycle of Life Chant

I'm a tiny seed, under the ground,
Sleeping, sleeping, surrounded by brown,
Brown, rich soil, warm and ready,
Ready to push and pop and sprout,
Here I come! I'm up and out!

Growing, growing, as I tall as I can,
Surrounded by blue and above the land,
I can see mountains and rain and snow,
And all of the seasons that come and go.

Winter and summer and spring and fall,
And fall is when I drop them all.
Pine cones thumping all around,
And dropping their seeds, under the ground.

Sleeping, sleeping, surrounded by brown,
Brown, rich soil, warm and ready,
Ready to push and pop and sprout,
Here I come! I'm up and out!

More Ideas:

Say this chant often during the fall. As the children begin to learn it, have them say the last word in each line before you say it.

Things to talk about:

1. Ask the question: "Does anyone know what the word 'mysterious' means?" Brainstorm! It could mean: something strange, something you can't explain, or something you can't figure out.
2. Provide examples to help explain mysterious. Make comments, such as, "There is a mysterious smell in the air." Everyone can cautiously sniff. "There is something mysterious-looking on my foot." Shake it off. Sit very still. Say: "I feel something mysterious is about to happen." Scream and jump.
3. Ask the question: "Has anyone ever seen or heard or felt anything mysterious?" It can be a smell, a feeling, something you have seen, or even a sound.

Materials:

A flashlight

Preparation: None

Things to do:

1. Introduce the season of fall in a mysterious way. Lower the lights. Sit together on the rug. Sit very still. Fall is a very mysterious month. Who would like to know why it is mysterious?
2. Sit on the rug with the children. Point out certain facts about fall. Below are some comments you might make:
   - It begins to get dark early. The days become shorter. The night is longer. Shine your flashlight around the room. Why do you think the days are shorter? (The sun does not shine on us as long.)
   - In the fall, the air begins to turn colder. What can we do? Wear warmer clothes. Turn the heater on in our house, and our school.
   - What happens to flowers in the fall? Some flowers will begin to dry out. They need warm weather to bloom.
   - Leaves will begin to dry out. Why? Trees need sunshine to grow and make green healthy leaves.

- Trees begin to drop things. In colder weather, they will drop pine cones, acorns, needles, leaves, and even their fruit. Why do they drop? Parts of the tree get very weak and dry. They can't hold on. Give everyone a small nut to hold. Hold it tight in your fist. You are a strong tree. Now you are getting cold and dry. Loosen your grip. What happens?
- You might feel the stirrings of a breeze. A fall breeze will blow leaves down a street. What else could a fall breeze do?

More Ideas:

- Make binoculars from paper rolls. Go outside. Walk around and try to find something that looks mysterious.
- Stand very still outside. Can you feel a small breeze? Can you see anything that the breeze is blowing?
- Take a paper bag and collect things that look dry. Have a circle time and share what you have found.

Things to talk about:

1. During each season, the earth looks a little different. What can change about the world around you? Brainstorm! Possible answers are: the weather, how trees look, the kind of animals that you might see, the birds that live in your area, the number of insects you might see, how the sky looks, and the outdoor colors.
2. Place a large box on the rug. Pretend the box is a treasure chest. In the chest, you are going to place things that remind you of each season. Ask the question: "What would you place in the chest to tell people about summer?" Possible answers might be: a beach ball, dolphins, sand, ocean water, suntan lotion, and a picture of the sun.
3. Now ask the question: "What would you place in the chest to remind people of fall." Answers might be: Different colored leaves, acorns, bark from trees, pictures of animals that live in woods, apples, pumpkin seeds, and pine cones.

Materials:

Orange posterboard, scissors, glue, collected outside items to make a wreath with

Preparation:

Cut a circle from posterboard. Cut a hole in the middle to make a wreath shape. Make a wreath for each child.

Things to do:

1. Go outside and collect fall items to make your wreath. You can also bring items from home: Collected items might be:
   - leaves, gold ribbon
   - acorns, weeds, and thistles
   - sunflower seeds, walnut halves
   - twigs, wildflowers
   - pine cones, red berries
   - bark, yellow yarn
2. Spread these items down the middle of table. Place glue and wreaths on the table.
3. Children can glue the fall items on a wreath.
4. When the wreaths have dried, hang them in the classroom or take them home.

More Ideas:

- Make a giant classroom wreath. Cut a large wreath shape from posterboard. Tape it on a wall. Glue on items throughout the week. You can hunt for the items or children can bring them from home.

Things to talk about:

1. Ask the questions: "What is a tree?" "Is it an animal?" "Is it a rock?" "Is it a human?" Brainstorm! It is a plant. It is the largest plant on the earth.
2. Trees are made up of different parts, just like we are. We have arms and legs and feet and ears. Name other parts. Then name parts of a tree. These might be: leaves, stems of leaves, branches, seeds, trunks, and even fruits and flowers. As parts are named, you can draw them on a large piece of butcher paper.
3. Why are trees terrific? Answers might be: They give us shade; They are fun to climb; They give us nuts and fruit; They give us wood for building houses; They give us wood for making paper; They send oxygen into the air; They add beauty to our world.
4. Who can describe a tree? Children can stand by the teacher and talk about a tree that they have seen.

Materials:

Paper, crayons, crepe paper

Preparation: None

Things to do:

1. Find a large tree. Stand around it and hold hands. Sing *Ring Around the Rosie.*
2. Make bark tracings. Give each child a sheet of paper. Go outside. Place your paper against the trunk of a tree. Rub over your paper with a crayon.
3. Celebrate a tree. Wrap crepe paper around the trunk. Tape heart pictures on the trunk. Play music. Dance around your tree.
4. Learn *The Tree Chant*. As you say the word "I," slap your thighs once. Pause one second. Then continue the verse with the following rhythm: Clap your hands twice. Cross your arms and slap your upper arms twice. Clap your hands again, twice. Then slap your thighs twice.

The Tree Chant

I went to climb a tree, tree, tree,
To see what I could see, see, see,
And all that I could see, see, see,
Was the top of the big green tree, tree, tree.

More Ideas:

- Say the chant slowly. Gradually increase your speed each time you say it.
- Have a child think of something you might see in a tree. Substitute this last line: Was a (*bird*) in the big green tree, tree, tree.
- Other words might be: apple, acorn, pine cone, squirrel, woodpecker, blue jay or cat.

Things to talk about:

1. Ask the question: "Who can tell me about themselves?" Brainstorm! Possible answers: age, where they live, who they live with, and what they like to do.
2. Now ask a child to stand near you. Ask the question: "Can you tell anything about (John) by looking at him?" Answers might include how he wears his hair, what type of clothes he might like, the color of his eyes, and how tall he is.
3. If you looked at a dog, what could you tell about the dog? Possible answers might be: What breed of dog it is, if it is a young or old dog, if it seems healthy or sick, if it is overfed or underfed, or if it needs a bath.

Materials:

Butcher paper, a felt pen, a picture of a large tree

Preparation:

Cut a large sheet of butcher paper. Draw a large circle on the paper. Draw concentric rings inside the circle. This is the top of an old, large tree stump. Draw some rings wider than others. Draw some rings with jagged edges. Shadow in some rings with a dark brown or black crayon. Draw holes on some rings.

Things to do:

1. Place the butcher paper on the rug. Sit around the tree rings. Dim the lights. Speak in soft tones. Establish a reverent atmosphere for this very old tree.
2. Show the picture of a large tree. What can this tree tell us about itself? Answers might be: if it has grown straight or leaning to one side, if it has leaves, if it is full-grown or thin and still growing, if it is green and healthy or dry and decayed, if it is a fruit tree, if it has pine cones on it.
3. Now explain that trees have information locked inside of them. Tree rings can reveal many things about the life of the tree.

4. Look at the tree rings. What can these rings tell us? Brainstorm! Possible answers are:
   - The rings tell us about weather conditions. In lean, dry years, the rings are thinner. The tree does not grow as thick and large.
   - In warm weather and abundant rainfall, the tree grows more and the rings are thicker. Find the lean years and the healthy years.
   - Insects can damage a tree. Find the rings that have holes in them. Which year or years were damaged by insects?
   - Fire can damage a tree. Look for the darker rings.
   - Human activities can damage a tree. People bore into trees to find minerals or extract sap. Look for jagged rings.
5. Sit quietly around the tree rings. Trees are the oldest living things on the earth. Some trees are a few thousand years old. If the tree could, what do you think it would tell us? Possible answers are: the types of cars it might have seen, the way people dress, changes in the environment, buildings built or knocked down, animals that have lived near the tree, roadways paved.

More Ideas:

- Draw the top of a tree stump for each child. Everyone can color in their tree rings. Sit together in a circle. Everyone can share their picture and tell a story about their tree. They can comment on what has happened to their tree and what it has seen.

Things to talk about:

1. Who has a birthday? Everybody. What does your birthday celebrate? It celebrates the day you were born.
2. Ask the children to tell you how old they are. If a child says four, you can say: "You have been on the earth four years."
3. Do animals have birthdays? Yes. An animal's birthday tells us how many years that animal has been alive.
4. Do trees have birthdays? We don't celebrate a tree's birthday, but we can tell how long a tree has been alive. How do you think we can tell the age of a tree? Brainstorm!
5. If you look at a tree stump, you can tell. You will see rings on the stump. Each ring represents a year. If the tree stump had 15 rings around it, how old was the tree?

Materials:

Butcher paper, tape, a felt pen

Preparation:

Cut a sheet of butcher paper. Tape it low on a wall. Draw a large circle on the paper.

Things to do:

1. Demonstrate how the rings grow. Draw a circle inside the circle, close to the edge. How old is the tree? One year old.
2. Continue to draw circles inside of each other. Stop as you reach the fifth circle. Then count them. The tree is now five years old. Stop again on the tenth circle and count them.
3. Stop and count them on the fifteenth and twentieth ring. How old was the tree when it fell or was cut down? Twenty years old.
4. What do you think happened to the tree? Possible answers might be: It was cut down for lumber; It was cut down to make paper; It grew very old and became weak; The land was cleared to build homes or highways; Lightening struck the tree.

More Ideas:

- Draw a tree stump for each child. The children can draw the inner rings inside their stump. When everyone has finished, count together the number of rings inside the stumps and determine the age of the trees.

Things to talk about:

1. Ask the question: "What is a recipe?" Possible answers are: It can tell you how to make something; It has instructions; It involves ingredients; A recipe can tell you how to make chocolate chip cookies.
2. There is something very special that trees make. What do you think it is? Brainstorm! The answer is sugar.
3. There are three things in the tree recipe that is needed to make sugar. Pretend you have a pot in front of you. Put in some sunlight. Pour in some water. Now blow into the pot. You have added the third ingredient - air. Stir it up. You have tree sugar.
4. What does the sugar do? It feeds the tree. It feeds the leaves, branches, trunk and roots. It keeps the leaves green.

Materials: None

Preparation: None

Things to do:

1. Explain that some fall or autumn trees lose their leaves. The leaves drop because their sugar supply has stopped. When the sugar is no longer in the leaf, the green color turns red, orange, yellow and gold.
2. Learn the following chant. Have everyone stand. Clap as you say the first three lines.
3. When you say the fourth line, drop to your knees.
4. Slowly bend down toward the rug, as you say the last two lines.
5. When you say the word gold, pop back up and clap your hands.

More Ideas:

- Say this chant slowly. As you learn it, say it faster and faster.
- If you can, collect autumn leaves and scatter them on the rug. As you say the word gold, throw them in the air.

Things to talk about:

1. Show a leaf. Ask the children: "What is this? Where do you think it came from? What color is it? What shape is it? Do you see anything else on this leaf? A stem? Veins? Points? Jagged edges?"
2. Now look at the leaf again. Use your imaginations. Ask the question: "What could we do with this leaf?" Brainstorm! Possible ideas are: Put it on your head for a hat; Tape it on a cut for a band-aid; Make a leaf eye patch; Wear it in your hair; Make a leaf boat; Wear it around your neck.
3. Say to the children "Everyone down on the rug. Close your eyes. Dream of a beautiful fall leaf. You can wake up when you feel a leaf brushing against your cheek."

Materials:

Leaves, glitter, glue, paper, wax paper, yarn, twigs, weeds, recorded music

Preparation:

Collect leaves.

Things to do:

1. Make leaf glitter. Crunch up dried autumn leaves. Sprinkle glitter on them. Mix them up. Spread glue or paste on a sheet of construction paper. Sprinkle on your leaf glitter.
2. Make leaf place mats. Cut out oblong shapes from wax paper. Place leaves on the oblong mats. Place an identical shape over the bottom shape. Iron them together. You can also glue, staple or thread them together with yarn.
3. Make leaf people. Place paper and glue on a table. Add yarn, twigs, weeds, and even dandelions. Design a leaf person.
4. Make a large leaf graph. Tape a long sheet of butcher paper on a wall. Draw graph lines on the paper. Collect many types of leaves. Tape leaves that match on different rows.
5. Play Hide a Leaf. Hide leaves around the classroom. Hunt for them. After the hunt, the children can share their leaf and describe it.
6. Do The Leaf Dance. Place a large leaf on the rug. Sit around the leaf. Play music. Everyone can take turns dancing around the leaf.
7. Make rainbow leaves. Glue green leaves on construction paper. Paint over the leaves with a variety of colors.

More Ideas:

- Take pictures of different types of leaves in your neighborhood. Tape them on a poster board.

Things to talk about:

1. What does the word sorting mean? Give examples. Your mom might say: Please sort the socks. What do you think that means? She might say: Put all your summer pajamas in one drawer and all your winter pajamas in another drawer. Sorting can mean placing similar items together and in different piles.
2. Have everyone observe the color of their socks. Sort everyone into "sitting," piles, with people who have matching sock colors.
3. How else can we sort ourselves. Brainstorm! Possible answers are: hairstyles, hair color, eye color, type of clothing and gender.

Materials:

A paper bag, white construction paper

Preparation:

Collect many types of leaves. Collect four or more different types. Examples might be: large, small, jagged, pointed, smooth, shiny, dull, or long. Place all the leaves in a large paper bag.

Things to do:

1. Sort the leaves. Place the paper bag on the rug. If you have collected five types of leaves, place five white sheets of paper on the rug.
2. Choose a child to be the leaf sorter. This child can select a leaf from the paper bag.
3. Ask the child to describe the leaf. Help with any adjectives. Is it smooth? Glossy? Does it have veins? Is it large or wide? Is it long and thin?
4. The child can now place the leaf on one of the white sheets of paper.
5. This child can now choose another leaf sorter to choose a leaf and describe it.
6. Continue until all the leaves have been sorted into their separate piles.

More Ideas:

- Before your circle time, go on a hunt with the children to collect the leaves.
- Scatter the leaves over the top of the table. Place a large sheet of butcher paper over the table, so it covers all of the leaves. Tape the sides down. Place crayons on the table. Demonstrate how to rub the crayons sideways to make leaf tracings.

Everlasting Leaves!

Things to talk about:

1. Ask the question: "What does it mean to preserve something?" Brainstorm! When you preserve something, you save it. You save its beauty. You keep it from getting old and crumbly and torn.
2. What kinds of things can you preserve? Possible answers are: You can dry flowers; You can dry leaves; You can preserve old letters and photographs; You can frame a special piece of embroidery or knitting; You can coat a painting with a special shellac; You can preserve jams and jellies.
3. Is there anything that you have that you would like to preserve?

Materials:

Fall leaves, paper, paint, a sharp knife, glycerin, string, a measuring cup, hot water, and a jar or pitcher

Preparation:

Collect fall leaves. Also, collect a large spray of leaves that are connected to their stems.

Things to do:

1. Preserve the shape of leaves with paint prints. Follow the directions below:

- Place the fall leaves on a table. Paint the underside of the leaves, starting from the middle line and painting outward.
- Place the leaves, paint-side down, on a piece of paper. Place another sheet of paper over the leaves. Press down.
- Carefully lift off the paper. Peel back the painted leaves.
- Observe the beautiful leaf prints.

2. Preserve fall leaves. They will darken slightly, but will remain natural looking. Follow the directions below:

- In a large jar, mix together $1\frac{1}{2}$ pints of hot water and $\frac{1}{2}$ pint of glycerin.
- Cut a slit at the end of each stem.
- Place the leaf branches in the jar.
- When the leaves slightly darken, take them out of the jar and tie them together with the string.
- Hang them upside down, in a dark, dry place, until they are completely dry.
- Display them in a vase.

More Ideas:

- You can dry flowers with a similar technique. Go on a flower hunt. Find flowers that are almost fully open with long stems attached. Pull off any leaves from the stems. Tie the flowers together with a string or rubber band. Hang them upside-down in a cool place, away from sunlight. A garage is a good place. When they have dried, place them in a vase and observe how pretty they still look.

Things to talk about:

1. What is a flower? It is a plant. Show a flower. Point out the stem, leaves, petals, and the middle of the flower. This is where you will find seeds.
2. Where do we find flowers? Everywhere. All over the earth. Where have you seen flowers growing? In your yard? In a field? On bushes? In your house?
3. What colors are flowers? Brainstorm! They come in every color. Think of as many colors as you can.
4. Why do you think people like flowers? Possible answers are: They are pretty; They add beauty to the earth; They add beauty to your home; You can wear them on your clothes or in your hair; Some people make leis out of flowers and wear them around their neck.

Materials: None

Preparation: None

Things to do:

1. Sit in a circle. Tell "The Flower Story." The story will explain how flowers are found all over the earth.
2. Act out the story. Below are suggestions for body movement:

- To be a happy flower, smile and wiggle your body.
- Hug yourself when you say, "loved being yellow."
- Fluff your hair when you say, "beautiful."
- Slowly droop down for growing old.
- Weave back and forth to make the wind.
- Wiggle your fingers in the air for scattering seeds.
- Cover the seeds with soil. Hold up a finger to show a plant that has emerged from the ground.
- Make a fist for a bud.
- Open your fist and spread fingers to form a flower.

The Flower Story

In the fall, there was a happy little flower named Fran.
Fran was yellow. She loved being yellow. Yellow was the color of the warm sun. Fran made everyone smile as they walked by her.
But one day, Fran realized that she had grown old.
She still felt happy. She had made many people smile.
Then a wind came blowing by. The wind gently shook Fran.
And Fran's seeds scattered all over the ground. Some of her seeds blew across the street.
Fran's seeds became covered by the soil. The sun kept her seeds warm.
When it rained, they grew. After awhile, they pushed themselves above the ground. Now they were tiny plants. Eventually, they grew bigger and bigger, and tiny buds formed. These buds opened into flowers.
These flowers were yellow. They were Fran's children. People smiled at them.
One day, the lady across the street, looked down, and there was a yellow flower in her yard.
"How did you get here?" she asked. "Well," she said, "I'm glad you're here. You are very beautiful to look at." And she smiled.

More Ideas:

- Make yellow flowers to use in the story. Cut the flower shapes above from yellow paper. Tape them on the end of green pipe cleaners.
- Plant yellow sunflowers.

The Flower Garden Chant

Things to talk about:

1. Ask the questions: "What is a garden?" "Does anyone have a garden?" "What grows in your garden?"
2. Why do you think people have gardens? Brainstorm! Possible answers are: to grow your own food, to add an attractive look to your yard, to grow certain flowers or vegetables and sell them, to work outside. Some people enjoy digging in the dirt.
3. What can you find in a garden, if you look very closely? Answers might be: butterflies, dragonflies, rolly-pollys, caterpillars, tomato bugs, beetles, and snails.
4. If you had a garden, what would you like to grow in it?

Materials: None

Preparation: None

Things to do:

1. Sing the following chant to the tune of *Lazy Mary Will You Get Up*. Clap as you sing it. When you say the word, surprise, throw your hands in the air.
2. Before you repeat the verse, the child on the teacher's left names a type of flower. If the child says *a rose*, add the words, *a rose*, after the word buttercup.
3. Point to each child as you say the name of their flower.
4. When you say the last verse, you will be saying the name of each flower mentioned.
5. Suggested flowers might be: a daisy, a daffodil, a sunflower, a dandelion, a tulip, a poppy, a lily, a pansy, a marigold, and a snapdragon.
6. The chant might be:

More Ideas:

- Before you begin the song, think of the name of a vegetable. To add some fun at the end, sing one last verse. Substitute the last line for the following: Surprise! A potato. What's a potato doing in my flower garden?

Things to talk about:

1. When you are hungry, what do you do? Brainstorm! Possible answers might be: Ask someone for a snack; Open up your refrigerator; Eat lunch; Go to a restaurant; Buy something at a market; Order pizza.
2. What do animals do when they are hungry? Possible ideas are: A pet might ask you for a treat; A pet will wait for you to feed it; A wild animal has to hunt for its food; Many animals have to search for food every day.
3. Some animals look for food in the fall, before the weather gets too cold. They store their food in safe places. Then, in winter, they dig their food up. Why would it be hard to find food in cold weather? Answers might be: Plants are covered by snow; Fruits and vegetables do not grow well in cold weather; Lakes can turn to ice; Some animals eat other animals.

Materials:

Acorns, at least one for each child. If you cannot find acorns, use walnuts or peanuts

Preparation:

Hide the acorns around the classroom.

Things to do:

1. Pretend to be squirrels. Curl up on the rug. Wake up from a nap. Stretch.
2. The teacher can now pretend to be the mother (or father) squirrel, asking the "squirrel," children this question: "Who remembers why I want you to search for acorns and bury them in the ground?"
3. On the count of three, the squirrel children can hunt around the room for the acorns.
4. When a child finds an acorn, he or she can find a spot in the classroom to hide it. Encourage everyone to remember where they have hidden their food.
5. When everyone has hidden their acorn, return to the rug. Curl up again. When you wake up, it will be winter.
6. Everyone can now go and find the acorn that they have hidden.

More Ideas:

- Hide nuts that you can eat together, after you have found your hidden treasures.
- Buy a variety of nuts. Hide them around the classroom. Bring them back to the rug and sort them.

Things to talk about:

1. Ask the question: "Pretend that you love candy bars. All of a sudden, there will be no more candy bars for a long time. What would you do?" Buy a lot of them. Store them away. Eat only one a day.
2. What do you think bears do, when they sense that cold weather is coming, and they won't be able to find a lot of food? Brainstorm!
3. After bears eat a tremendous amount of food, and store fat in their bodies to keep them warm, they go into a deep sleep. That is called hibernation.
4. Where do you think bears hibernate? someplace warm, a place where they will not be disturbed, a safe place where people or wild animals will not bother them.

Materials: None

Preparation: None

Things to do:

1. Mention that many animals hibernate. Some animals sleep through the winter months, without waking. Some animals sleep for awhile, wake up and eat, and go back to sleep. Which type of animal would you rather be?
2. Name different animals that hibernate. As you name them, pretend to be that animal.
3. Then mention the type of dwelling they find to hibernate in. Pretend to dig or hide in sleep in the manner of that particular animal.
4. Suggested animals and their resting places are listed below:
   - Bears sleep in dens.
   - Raccoons sleep in a hollow log.
   - Gophers dig holes.
   - Beavers build lodges.
   - Snakes sleep in-between rocks.
   - Frogs sleep at the bottom of ponds.
   - Turtles sleep at the bottom of streams.
   - Bats sleep in warm buildings or caves.
   - Ladybugs hide under bark.

More Ideas:

- Repeat the animals names and their resting places a few times. Then say only the name of the animal. See if the children can remember the place that they hibernate in.

Things to talk about:

1. Would you rather be an animal that is someone's pet, or would you rather be a wild animal that lives outside? Why?
2. List animals that live outside, especially those that prepare for colder weather. These animals might be: frogs, snakes, turtles, bears, squirrels, and chipmunks. (Act out the animals to help the children guess.)
3. Which animal would you like to be, that prepares for winter months or that hibernates?
4. How do you think animals know that colder weather is coming? Brainstorm! Do they have a calendar that they look at? Did someone tell them? Can they sense it?

Materials: None

Preparation: None

Things to do:

1. Sing the following song to the tune of *Where is Thumbkin?* Place your hands behind your back. Bring out both thumbs for the first verse. Continue using each set of fingers until you reach your pinkies.
2. For the last verse, bring out all your fingers and wiggle them.

Where is brown bear?

Where is brown bear?
Where is brown bear?
Here I am!
Here I am!
In the chilly weather,
Do you think we better,
Hibernate,
Hibernate.

Where is chipmunk?
Where is chipmunk?
Here I am!
Here I am!
In the chilly weather,
Do you think we better,
Hibernate,
Hibernate.

Where is turtle?
Where is turtle?
Here I am!
Here I am!
In the chilly weather,
Do you think we better,
Hibernate,
Hibernate.

Where is little frog?
Where is little frog?
Here I am!
Here I am!
In the chilly weather,
Do you think we better,
Hibernate,
Hibernate.

Where is everybody?
Where is everybody?
Here we are?
Here we are?
In the chilly weather,
Do you think we better,
Hibernate,
Hibernate.

More Ideas:

- Cut large sheets of butcher paper. Tape them around the room, to form places the children can crawl under. These are your bear caves! Pretend to sleep inside them. Hibernate!
- As an option, use sheets to make caves with.

Bears in The Woods

Things to talk about:

1. Do bears have families? Who would be in a bear family? How do you think bears meet? Does someone introduce them? Do they meet at a party? Do they meet in the woods?
2. If you were a bear, what would you like to do? Brainstorm! Possible answers are: Climb trees; Hunt for food; Play with a friend bear; Play in a stream; Eat honey and berries; Sleep in a cave; or, hibernate.
3. Why do you think people write songs about bears? Songs can help us learn about different things, including bears. We celebrate events with songs. We sing songs just for fun.

Materials: None

Preparation: None

Things to do:

Ask the questions: "Who wants to see if there are bears in the woods?" "If you saw a bear in the woods, what would you do?"

1. Sit together on the rug. Learn the following chant. Slap your thighs in a walking motion to establish a rhythm. Do this for the first three lines in each verse. When you say the words, "Way, way, over there," point in front of you, four times.
2. Place your finger on your lips to make the "Shh" sound.
3. Now growl. After you growl, move yourself backward very quietly. Then slap your hands on your thighs and run away.

Bear in the Woods

Who's that walking in the deep-dark woods?
Who's that walking in the deep-dark woods?
Who's that walking in the deep-dark woods?
Way, way, over there,
Shh! Shh! It's papa bear!
(loud growl)

Who's that walking in the deep-dark woods?
Who's that walking in the deep-dark woods?
Who's that walking in the deep-dark woods?
Way, way, over there,
Shh! Shh! It's mama bear!
(medium growl)

Who's that walking in the deep-dark woods?
Who's that walking in the deep-dark woods?
Who's that walking in the deep-dark woods?
Way, way, over there,
Shh! Shh! It's baby bear!
(tiny growl)

More Ideas:

- Choose three children to pretend to be The Three Bears. As you chant about each bear, the assigned bear can growl to frighten you.

Wind Experiments

Things to talk about:

1. Ask the question: "What is the wind?" Brainstorm! The air around us is always on the move. When you can feel it, we call it a wind.
2. Can you see the wind? No, but you can see what the wind does. How? You can see the wind move leaves, tree branches, push paper across a street, and blow your hair.
2. Where can you feel a wind? Possible answers are: There are winds in mountains, in valleys, over oceans, in deserts, over towns, in fields, and in your backyard.
3. Sit very still. Can you feel a wind now? Only if the door or windows are open. Why? Winds are outside.
4. Name different types of winds. A wind can become a breeze, a strong wind, a tornado, a hurricane, a typhoon, a gale, or a waterspout.
5. If you were a wind, where would you like to go?

Materials:

Crepe paper, construction paper, paper clips, paper bags

Preparation:

See below.

Things to do:

1. Do a wind experiment. This experiment will allow you to see wind all over your playground. Do this on a windy day. Cut crepe paper into long strips. Tie as many as you can around the playground. Tie them from tree branches, playground equipment, and parts of the outside building. Tie them so they dangle down. If you have a monkey bar, tie them all the way across to form a wall of paper. Stand back and observe. Your playground will look amazing.

2. Make windmills. Everyone can color a square of paper. Then fold each square of paper, corner to opposite corner. Open up the paper and you will see two diagonal lines, making an X across the paper. Cut half way along each line, from each corner. Fold each alternate corner to the center and tape it down. Attach this to a straw with a paper clip. Hold them up and watch them spin.
3. Try to catch the wind. Go outside with small paper bags. Everyone can run and try to catch the wind inside their bag. Then fold the top down on your bag, and trap the wind inside. Bring your wind bags back to the classroom. Sit together on the rug. Everyone can dump out their wind on the rug. Where is it? Where did it go? Talk about how the wind is invisible, but you can see things that is does. The wind needs to be moving. The wind moves outside.
4. Take pictures of things the wind is moving. Post them on a board. Think of a title for your board, such as, Watch the Wind or Wind Pictures.
5. Make balloon kites. Blow up balloons. Tie the end on a long string. Run outside and hold your arm up high. Do a wind dance. Tie crepe paper streamers on your arms. Play music. Dance with the wind.

More Ideas:

- Give everyone wind homework. Ask each child to go outside their house with a parent and observe the wind. Have a parent write down all the things that the wind is moving. The next day, have a wind share. Read everyone's account of their wind findings.

Things to talk about:

1. What is the moon? Brainstorm! The moon is the closest celestial object in our sky. It is a solid object, similar to a large chuck of rock. You can stand on it.
2. How big is the moon? Demonstrate. Hold up a soccer ball, or a ball of the same size. Now hold up an orange. Pretend the ball is the earth. The orange is the moon. Which is bigger - the earth or the moon?
3. Why does the moon look so bright at night? It reflects the light from the sun. If the earth didn't have a bright moon, would the night be lighter or darker?
3. Is there any life on the moon? Some people think there could be. Other people say no. There is no air or water on the moon. What do you think?

Materials:

Butcher paper, scissors, tape, flashlight

Preparation:

Cut a large moon from the butcher paper. Tape the moon low on a wall.

Things to do:

1. Sit in front of the moon. Explain that it is a harvest moon. You see a harvest moon in the fall. The harvest moon is a full moon.
2. Lower the lights. Shine a flashlight on the moon. Many people enjoy looking at the moon. Why do you think it makes people feel good to look at the moon? How does it make you feel?
3. The moon shines on everything. Everyone, in turn, can stand in front of the moon. Each child can say the following sentence and fill in the blank: The moon shines on (trees!)
4. Do a moon dance. Play gentle music. Keep the lights low. Shine the flashlight on the moon. Everyone can dance under the moon.

More Ideas:

- Some people see a man in the moon. It could be the craters that look like a face. What do you think? Give everyone a felt marker and paper. Each child, in turn, can draw a man in the moon.

Things to talk about:

1. Ask the question: “What is a pattern?” Brainstorm! A pattern is a special design. Look for patterns on your clothes. Look for patterns in the classroom border designs or floor tiles.
2. How could you make a people pattern? Have every other child raise their arm. What is the pattern? How else can we make a people pattern?
3. There are patterns in nature. What kind of patterns might you see outside? Possible answers are: patterns in clouds, spots on a ladybug, stripes on a bee, designs on a butterfly wing, and feathers on a bird.
4. Do spiders make patterns? How? A web is a pattern. Different types of spiders build different webs.
5. If you were a spider, what would your web look like?

Materials:

Black construction paper, glue, white yarn, brushes, scissors

Preparation:

Cut the yarn into strings. Make at least 10 strings for each child.

Things to do:

1. Show pictures of spider webs. If you can, collect one.
2. Draw spider webs on a blackboard.
3. Place black paper, glue and strings of yarn on a table. Everyone can brush their strings with glue. Then they can place their strings of yarn, in a web design, on the black paper.
4. When the webs have dried, tape them on a wall. Label the wall: No Two Webs Are Alike!

More Ideas:

- Pretend to be a wolf spider. Drape a white sheet over a table. Have fun throwing a skein of white or silver yarn, back and forth, over the table. Play inside your spider tent.

Things to talk about:

1. Who likes spiders? Why? Why not? Spiders are good for the earth. They help keep the insect population down. Without spiders, there might be too many flies.
2. Where do spiders live? They live anywhere they can weave a web. Brainstorm where you might see a web.
3. Spiders can do something that we can't. What is it? They have special organs in their abdomen that spin their silky threads. Push hard with your stomach muscles. No matter how hard we push, we will never be able to spin a web.
4. Why do spiders built webs? They catch their food in webs. They live in their webs.
5. Why do you think spiders often have to build a new web every day? Their web can easily get torn or broken? How would this happen? Possible answers are: People often destroy webs in their homes; A rainstorm can damage a web; A dog can walk by and brush against a web.

Materials:

A skein of white or silver yarn, black construction paper, scissors, tape

Preparation:

Draw and cut out a spider from black paper.

Things to do:

1. Build a giant spider web. Begin by tying one end of the yarn to a sturdy piece of furniture or object.
2. Walk the skein to a different place in the room. Wrap it around another object, at least 10 feet away. Continue to walk the yarn around the web area, weaving back and forth and in-between. Bring the yarn over and under each other.
3. Make the web while the children sit and watch. As an option, you can hand the skein to each child and have them weave a part of it.
4. When you have woven a giant web, tape the paper spider somewhere on the web.
5. Sit around the giant spider web. Take turns crawling under the web and standing up inside of it. Go slowly. Weave yourself in and out. Try not to touch the web.

More Ideas:

- Have everyone lay down under the web. Look up into the design. Lay very still. How would you feel if you were an insect caught in a web?
- Give everyone at least three feet of yarn. The children can weave their on webs around the classroom.

Have them take their yarn home and build a web.

Along Came a Spider

Things to talk about:

1. How does a spider get her food? Does she go to a spider store? Does she make noises that attract insects to herweb? A spider hides somewhere on her web or even under a nearby leaf. She keeps a thread of the web attached to her.
2. When an insect lands on her web, how do you think the spider knows? The web shakes. She can feel it. What do you think she does next? She moves fast and attacks the insect.
3. Now what does she do? She eats the insect. If she doesn't feel like eating it, she will wrap it up with threads and save it for later.
4. A spider only eats insects. If you ate only one thing, every day, what would it be? Brainstorm!

Materials:

A toy spider, yarn, scissors, a chair

Preparation:

Cut a string of yarn, tie it on the spider.

Things to do:

1. Play The Little Miss Muffet game. Place a chair on the rug. Have everyone sit in front of the chair. Choose a child to be either Miss Muffet or Mister Muffet.
2. This child can sit in the chair. Now choose a child to be the spider. The spider stands behind the child who is sitting, and holds the dangling spider.
3. Say the following chant. When you finish the chant, the child with the spider can dangle the toy spider in front of the "chair," person's face. Try to scare this person. If they are scared, they might have a chance to jump off the web and avoid being eaten.

Little Miss Muffet,
Sat on her tuffet,
Eating her curds and whey.

Along came a spider,
And sat down beside her,
And frightened Miss Muffet away!

4. The children can take turns being Miss or Mister Muffet and the spider.
5. As an option, you can place a pillow on the chair for the tuffet.

More Ideas:

- Everyone can draw and cut out a spider from black construction paper. Tape yarn to your spiders and attach the free end to a straw. Bring your dangling spiders home.

Things to talk about:

1. In the fall, days grow shorter and colder. Is it dark or light when you wake up? It should be lighter in the morning. What might happen if it gets lighter, earlier in the morning? Brainstorm! Possible answers are: You might wake up earlier; Your bedroom will get lighter at an earlier hour; You might eat breakfast sooner; You might hear birds chirping earlier; Your pets might wake up earlier and stretch, yawn or wake you to go out.
2. If it gets darker earlier in the evening, what might happen? You might have to go inside your house sooner, if you are playing outside; You might eat dinner sooner; You might get in your pajamas sooner; You might feel sleepy early in the evening.
3. Do animals sense the change in the fall days? Yes. They notice the weather and how much food there is for them to find.
4. What do some animals do before the weather gets very cold and food is scarce. They migrate. What does that mean? Some birds and animals will travel great distances, leaving their homes, to find a place to live where the weather is warmer and there is plenty of food.
5. We don't have to migrate to stay warm and have enough eat. How do we prepare for cold weather?

Materials:

Yellow construction paper, a marker, scissors, tape

Preparation:

Draw and cut out a large sun from yellow paper. Tape the sun on a wall.

Things to do:

1. Divide the class into three groups. These groups can be reindeer, butterflies and swallows. As an option, place stickers on each group to show what they are.
2. Observe the sun on the wall. The sun represents a place that has warmer weather. Make up a name for this place, such as, Sun City.
3. Choose a child, from each group, to be the leader. Each child can lead their migrating group of animals to Sun City. Encourage creative pathways while migrating. Go under tables, around chairs and jump over imaginary rivers.
4. Each group can take turns to avoid migrating traffic jams. If you have the time, take turns being the leader.

More Ideas:

- Extend your migrating to outside. Find fun pathways to a warm weather spot.

Things to talk about:

1. If you took a family vacation, and you drove to a place far away, how would you know how to get there? Answers might be: You could follow a map; Someone gave you directions; You have been there before and you remember how to get there.
2. Some birds migrate to warmer climates at the beginning of fall. They travel together in flocks. They fly hundreds of miles. Sometimes they don't stop to eat or drink. How do they survive? They eat many insects during the summer. They store food and water inside their bodies, in their body fat.
3. How do you think birds know how to get to their destination? Brainstorm. Do they have a bird map? Do they follow an airplane? It is a mystery. No one knows for sure. Some people think that they follow landmarks on the earth, such as rivers and mountains, or even the sun. At night, what could birds follow? They might follow the stars and the moon.

Materials:

A brown blanket, blue butcher paper or construction paper, yellow butcher or construction paper, green butcher paper or white paper, a white sheet, tape, and scissors

Preparation:

Drape the blanket over three chairs. This is your mountain range. Place a long strip of blue paper on the rug or floor for your river. Place a round circle of blue paper on the rug for your lake. Place a sheet on the rug for snow. Build houses with blocks for your town. Place a sheet of yellow paper on the rug for a desert. Tape a green sheet of butcher paper on a wall, or draw tall trees on a large sheet of paper for your forest.Tape all the paper down.

Things to do:

1. Sit together on the rug. Pretend to be a flock of migrating birds. You can be swallows. Swallows migrate thousands of miles.
2. Everyone can stand and stretch their wings. Then take off. Follow a path that has been set up. The teacher can offer directions that will help keep the swallows on their long journey to a warmer land. Make sure you have chosen a warm, designated spot to land.
4. Below is a suggested path and landmarks that you can fly over:

- Fly around the mountain range.
- Fly over the river.
- Fly over the lake.
- Fly over the desert.
- Fly over the snow.
- Fly around the town.
- Fly by the forest.

5. As the swallows complete their course, they can land and rest in their new home.

More Ideas:

- You can have each child, in turn, follow the map.
- Play soft music while everyone migrates. Mention that it is quiet high up in the sky as the birds fly.

Things to talk about:

1. Who has felt very, very cold? What made you feel cold? Where were you when you were feeling cold?
2. Now ask the question: "What can you do when you feel cold?" Brainstorm! Possible answers might be: You put on a coat; You put on a hat; You put on socks or bedroom slippers; You closed a door or window; You might hug yourself or stand near another person.
3. Ask the questions: "Do animals get cold?" "What can animals do to feel warmer?" Answers might be: They can crawl inside a cave; They can burrow under the ground; They can rest behind a tree or a large rock; They can huddle together; They can grow a thick coat as protection from cold weather.
4. If you could grow a long thick coat of fur to stay warm, what color would it be?

Materials:

Butcher paper, scissors, tape, a felt marker, glue, cotton balls

Preparation: None

Things to do:

1. Draw a large rabbit on the white butcher paper.
2. Spray or brush glue over the entire rabbit.
3. Empty bags of white cotton balls on the rug.
4. Choose children, a few at a time, to stick the cotton balls on the rabbit.
5. When the rabbit is covered with cotton balls, observe your winter rabbit. Notice how thick his coat is. Touch it. Do you think it will keep him warm in very cold weather?

More Ideas:

- Draw rabbits on individual sheets of paper. Everyone can make their own winter rabbit to take home.

Things to talk about:

1. Rabbits do well in cold weather, but they still need three things to survive! What are they? Brainstorm! Rabbits need food, water and shelter from extreme weather, such as, cold winds and rain.
2. Do you think rabbits need to eat more or less during cold weather? More! If a rabbit shivers, because of the cold, he is using up body heat. Like exercise, the shivers will burn fat and calories. Everyone shiver! If you shivered all day, you might lose weight!
3. Why do you think the fur on some rabbits turns white during the winter? Camouflage! How does this help the rabbit survive? Hunters have a hard time seeing a white rabbit sitting on white snow! Animals that eat rabbits have a hard time, also.

Materials: Butcher paper

Preparation: None

Things to do:

1. Place a large sheet of butcher paper on the rug. Pretend it is snow! Now pretend you are white rabbits. Sit very still on the snow. Don't move! There is danger coming!
2. Play The Camouflage Game! Have everyone stand. Play music. The Freeze Dance can work for this game! When the music stops, everyone can camouflage. Stand very still. If the teacher sees you move, a fox has eaten you!

3. Learn the following chant. Use the same rhythm as *Little Rabbit Foo-Foo*. Do the following movements:

- Hide your hand behind your back to begin. Move your hand out with two fingers up for rabbit ears. Hop your hand across your body for the first verse.
- Use your other hand to be the fox. Move thumb and fingers up and down to make the fox talk.
- Have this hand slap the rabbit hand when you say the word bop!
- After you say run and hide, slap your thighs and run!
- Continue these movements through the last run.
- After the last run, sit very still. Then use a lower fox, voice and say: I can't see you, where did you go?
- Use a higher pitched voice to respond, using the rabbits words in the verse.
- Sit still for a few seconds, until you feel the fox has left.

Little Rabbit Bo-Bo

Little rabbit bo-bo,
Hopping in the snow, snow,
Looking for some food,
And wondering where to go!

And along came a white fox,
And he said:

Little rabbit bo-bo,
Hiding in the snow, snow,
I'm going to catch you,
And bop you on the head!
I'll give you three more chances,
To run and hide!

Little rabbit bo-bo,
Hopping in the snow, snow,
Looking for some food,
And wondering where to go!

And along came a white fox,
And he said:

Little rabbit bo-bo,
Hiding in the snow, snow,
I'm going to catch you,
And bop you on the head!
I'll give you two more chances,
To run and hide!

Little rabbit bo-bo,
Hopping in the snow, snow,
Looking for some food,
And wondering where to go!

And along came a white fox,
And he said:

Little rabbit bo-bo,
Hiding in the snow, snow,
I'm going to catch you,
And bop you on the head!
I'll give you one more chance,
To run and hide!

Little rabbit bo-bo,
Hopping in the snow, snow,
Looking for some food,
And wondering where to go!

And along came a white fox,
And he said:

Little rabbit bo-bo,
Hiding in the snow, snow,
I'm going to catch,
You and bop you on the head!
No more chances!
Run!

Finally, the fox said:
I can't see you!
Where did you go?

I'm camouflaged,
And hiding in
the snow!

Things to talk about:

1. Ask the question: "What is a pumpkin?" Brainstorm! Possible answers: It is a vegetable; It grows from a pumpkin seed; It grows on vines; It can be different colors, such as, dark orange, light orange, and white.
2. What do people do with pumpkins? Possible answers are: They decorate their homes with pumpkins; They make pumpkin pie; They make pumpkin bread; They make pumpkin cookies; They sell pumpkins at their pumpkin farms.
3. How do you turn a pumpkin into a jack-o'-lantern? You carve a face on it. How do you carve a face on a pumpkin? You cut off the top, to make a lid. You scoop out the insides. You use a sharp knife to carve a face. You put a candle inside the pumpkin. You put the lid on. Turn off the lights and watch your glowing jack-o'-lantern.
4. Who can repeat this process?

Materials:

A large and small pumpkin, orange balloons, markers, paper bags, newspaper, yarn, orange paint

Preparation: None

Things to do:

1. Carve a pumpkin. Each child can help scoop out the insides. When you have finished, sit around your jack-o'-lantern and makeup pumpkin stories.
2. Play Hot Potato Pumpkin. Sit in a circle. The teacher holds a small pumpkin. Quickly pass the pumpkin around the circle. As you pass the pumpkin, say over and over again: Hot-Potato Pumpkin. The teacher can choose when to say the word "Pop!" The child holding the pumpkin, when the teacher says "Pop," rolls the pumpkin across the circle. The nearest child can grab the pumpkin. Continue with the chant.
3. Stuff small paper bags with shredded newspaper. Twist the top for a pumpkin stem. Tie it with green yarn. Spray or paint the bags orange. When they have dried, paint faces on them. Take your jack-o'-lantern bags home.

More Ideas:

- Bake large pumpkin cookies, at least one for each child. The children can frost their cookies and paint faces on them. Use small frosting tubes to make jack-o'-lantern faces.

Things to talk about:

1. Talk about The Great Wise Pumpkin Legend. Some people say there is a Great Wise Pumpkin that can only be seen on Halloween. What do you think he looks like?
2. The Great Wise Pumpkin lives in pumpkin patches. He is only visible at night. If you went looking for him, what would you take with you. Brainstorm! Possible answers might be: a flashlight, a snack, a camera; a jacket, maybe a friend.
3. If you find The Great Wise Pumpkin, you can ask him a question. What would you ask him? Brainstorm!

Materials:

A pumpkin, a large sheet or blanket

Materials: None

Preparation: None

Things to do:

1. Sit in a circle. Place a pumpkin in the middle of the circle.
2. Ask the question: "Who would like to be The Great Wise Pumpkin?" A child, who volunteers, can sit in the middle of the circle, with the pumpkin in his or her lap.
3. Drape the sheet or blanket over the child's back and around the shoulders.
4. Now this child has become The Great Wise Pumpkin. Everyone can take turns asking The Great Wise Pumpkin a question.
5. When questions have finished, The Great Wise Pumpkin can pass the pumpkin to another child. Now that child becomes The Great Wise Pumpkin.

More Ideas:

- Dim the lights. Use a flashlight and walk quietly around the classroom. Try to find The Great Wise Pumpkin. The child, who is The Great Wise Pumpkin, can be sitting somewhere in the classroom. When you find The Great Wise Pumpkin, sit around him or her and ask your questions.

Things to talk about:

1. When you knock on someone's door on Halloween night, what do you say? Trick or treat! What does that mean? Think about it.
2. What is your favorite part of Halloween? Is it wearing a costume? Is it knocking on doors? Is it dumping out all your candy and looking at it? Brainstorm!
3. Talk about rules to follow for a safe and fun night. Below are some suggestions to talk about:

- Bring a flashlight. You might need some extra light. It's easy to trip or fall over objects in the dark.
- Cross a street only at the street corner. Why? Cars stop at corners.
- Only go to lit houses. A house without any lights usually means: Please don't disturb us.
- Write your name and number on your costume. If you get lost, an adult can call your home.
- Travel in groups. You will be safer if you are not alone.
- Do not eat any candy until you get home. Your parents will be able to tell if there is anything in your bag that is harmful to eat.

Materials:

A posterboard, a marker, scissors, a candy kiss and small paper bag, one for each child

Preparation:

Draw a large door on the posterboard. Add a doorknob.

Things to do:

1. Practice trick-or-treating. Sit in a circle. Give everyone a paper bag.
2. The teacher can sit in a chair and hold up the posterboard door.
3. Now choose a child to be the trick-or-treater. This child can stand, knock on the door, and say: Trick-or-treat!
4. The teacher can then put down the door and give the child a candy kiss.
5. Give each child a turn to be the trick-or-treater.

More Ideas:

- Do it again. This time, play a trick on each child. A trick could be: Wiggling a rubber snake or spider, after you put the door down.

Things to talk about:

1. Ask children to use their imaginations. Hold up a page of stickers. Ask the question: "What are these?" Then ask: "What could we do with all these stickers?" Brainstorm! Possible answers might be: Put them on your clothes; Put them on paper; Put them on your skin; Decorate a notebook; Share them with friends.
2. It is fun and easy to make up games. What kind of games could we play with these stickers? Answers might be: A matching game; Hide the stickers and try to find them; Act out a certain sticker; Give clues and guess which sticker you are thinking about.
3. If you could become one of these stickers, which one would you be? Why?

Materials:

Halloween stickers, posterboard, a marker, paper, crayons, envelopes (one for each child), pennies (two for each child)

Preparation:

Follow each game instruction.

Things to do:

1. Play a memory game. Place one sticker on index cards, making sure there are matches, at least one for each child. Place them, sticker-side down, on the rug. Take turns turning over two cards at a time to find matches.
2. Make Halloween crowns. Cut out crown shapes, one for each child. Paint or color the crowns black and orange. Decorate them with Halloween stickers.
3. Hunt for stickers. Hide stickers around the classroom. Then give everyone an envelope with one matching sticker inside. Everyone can open their envelope and hunt for its match.
4. Play a penny throw game. Draw horizontal and vertical lines on a posterboard. Place one sticker inside each square. Make sure there are many matches on the board. Give a child two pennies. This child can throw the pennies, one at a time, on the board. See if the pennies stop on matching stickers. Take turns throwing the pennies and trying to land on matches.
5. Make up stories about the stickers. Give everyone one or two stickers and a sheet of paper. Place crayons on the rug. Everyone can draw a picture, adding their stickers. The children can then stand, one by one, and tell a story about their drawing and their sticker.

More Ideas:

- Place a sticker on each child's hand. Use matching stickers. Everyone can then walk around and try to find the person who has a sticker, matching the one on their hand.

Broom Broom Zelda

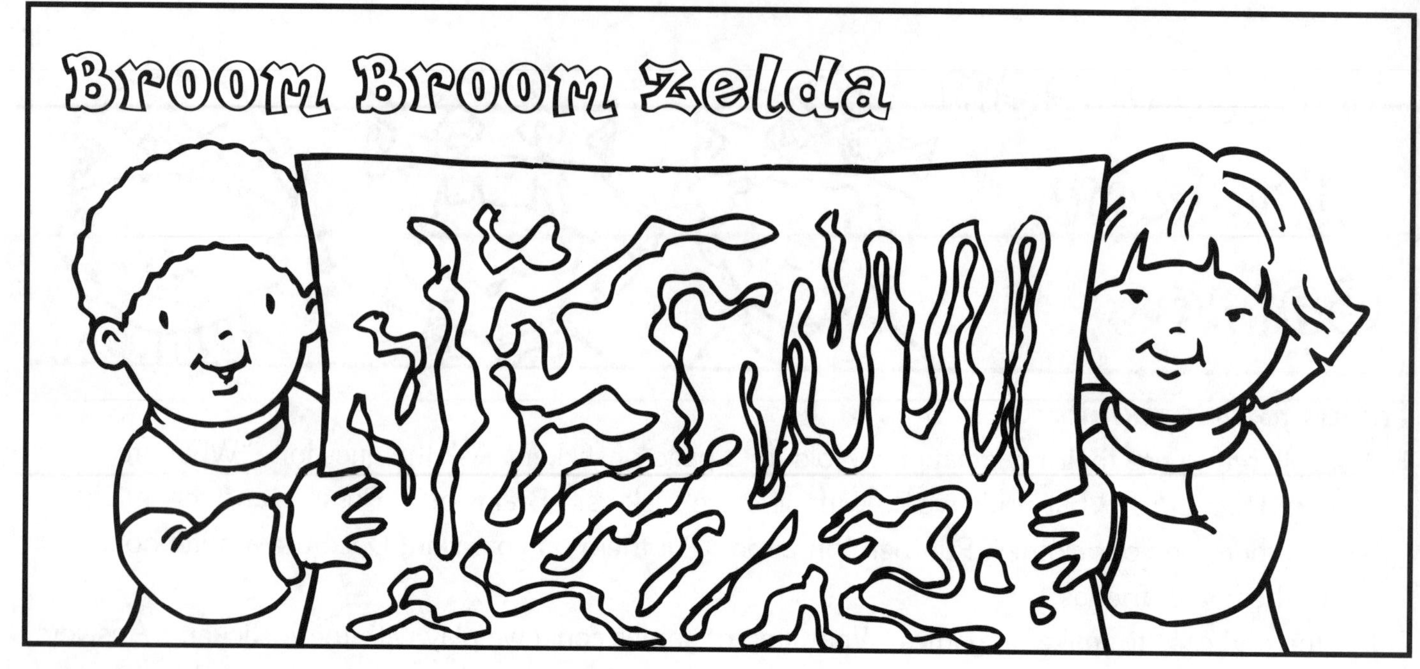

Things to talk about:

1. Show the children a broom. Ask what it is. Then ask the question: "What do you do with a broom?"
2. Ask for volunteers to demonstrate a sweeping motion. Sweep to music.
3. Ask the question: "Who rides on a broom?" A witch. "Why would a witch choose a broom to ride on, instead of an airplane?" Brainstorm!
4. If you rode on a broom, how would you position yourself? Ask for volunteers to demonstrate how they might sit on a broom and hold on.

Materials:
A broom, butcher paper, scissors, tape, paint

Preparation:

Cut a long strip of butcher paper. Tape it on the floor.

Things to do:

1. Tell the story of Broom Broom Zelda: Broom Broom Zelda was a witch. Children were afraid of Broom Broom Zelda. They were afraid of her magic broom. They would sing songs about her.
2. Now sing the first two verses to the tune *London Bridges*. Clap as you sing it.
3. After the two verses, the teacher yells "Stop!" The teacher then reads the following two verses.
4. The children then sing the last two verses to the tune of *London Bridge*.
5. When you have finished the song, squirt paint down the middle of the butcher paper. The children can take turns painting with Broom Broom Zelda's broom.
6. When the painting has dried, tape it on a wall. Label it Broom Painting.

Broom Broom Zelda

Broom Broom Zelda was a big bad witch,
A big bad witch,
A big bad witch,
Broom Broom Zelda was a big bad witch,
And everyone would sing.

Broom Broom Zelda was a big bad witch,
A big bad witch,
A big bad witch,
Broom Broom Zelda was a big bad witch,
And everyone would sing.

STOP!
There's something wrong with this song!
Broom Broom Zelda was not a big bad witch.
She was an itty bitty witch,
Only two feet tall!
And she didn't ride her broom,
At all!

She liked to paint with it!
So she asked all the children,
To paint with her broom,
And as they did,
They changed their tune:

Broom Broom Zelda was an itty bitty witch,
An itty bitty witch,
An itty bitty witch,
Broom Broom Zelda was an itty bitty witch,
Who wasn't mean at all!

Broom Broom Zelda was an itty bitty witch,
An itty bitty witch,
An itty bitty witch,
Broom Broom Zelda was an itty bitty witch,
Who wasn't mean at all!

More Ideas:

- What do you think Broom Broom Zelda looks like? Have everyone paint a picture of her. Tape the pictures by the broom painting.
- Sing the first verse of this song very slowly. Continue to sing the first verse, over and over, but increasing your speed each time!

Things to talk about:

1. Ask the question: "What is a ghost?" (You will get many interesting answers.)
2. Has anyone seen a ghost? What did it look like? Where did you see it?
3. If you could become a ghost, just for one night, what would you look like? What would you do? Brainstorm!
4. Would you be a friendly ghost or a scary ghost? Would you make a noise? What would it sound like?
5. What is a good name for a ghost? Spooky? Mr. Haunt? How about Boo!

Materials: None

Preparation: None

Things to do:

1. Sing the following ghostly songs. Follow the suggested movements:

SONG NUMBER ONE:

(This chant is similar to *Five Little Monkeys*.)

- For the first line in each verse: Fly your hand around, using a matching number of fingers to ghosts.
- For the second line in each verse: Fly your first finger behind your back.
- For the third and fourth lines in each verse: Hold up a palm. With your first finger, on your other hand, punch numbers in.
- For the fifth line: Wag your finger.
- For the sixth line: Spread fingers apart, with your palm down. Wiggle your fingers and slowly move your hand upward.
- For the last two lines, in the last verse, wag your finger.
- Then place hands over your head and crouch down. Jump back up and say, Boo!

Five Little Ghosts

Five little ghosts went flying all around.
One little ghost could not be found,
Mama called the sheriff,
And the sheriff said:
Keep those little ghosts,
Floating in their bed!

Four little ghosts went flying all around,
One little ghost could not be found,
Mama called the sheriff,
And the sheriff said:
Keep those little ghosts,
Floating in their bed!

Three little ghosts went flying all around,
One little ghost could not be found.
Mama called the sheriff,
And the sheriff said:
Keep those little ghosts,
Floating in their beds!

Two little ghosts went flying all around,
One little ghost could not be found.
Mama called the sheriff,
And the sheriff said:
Keep those little ghosts,
Floating in their beds!

One little ghost went flying all around,
He flew off and was not found.
Mama called the sheriff,
And the sheriff said:
I bet they're hiding,
Under the bed!
(BOO!)

SONG NUMBER TWO:

(Sing this to the tune of *London Bridge*)

- Make a bridge with one other child.
- Everyone can walk through the haunted house while you sing the song.
- Trap one or two children.
- As you end the song, moan like a ghost.

Haunted House Is Falling Down

Haunted house is falling down,
Falling down,
Falling down,
Haunted house is falling down,
Don't get trapped inside!

Caught you now and lock you in,
Lock you in,
Lock you in,
Caught you now and lock you in,
With all the moaning ghosts!

SONG NUMBER THREE:

(Say to the tune of *Patty-Cake*)

- For the first three lines: Clap your hands together, then slap your thighs. Repeat this four times.
- For the fourth and fifth lines: Bend an arm at the elbow for a pan. Stir with the other hand.
- For the sixth line: Grab handles with both fists and pretend to tilt a pan toward you.
- For the seventh line: Tap a fist finger, three times, on the other wrist.
- For the eighth line: Pretend to hold a plate, with both hands.
- For the last line: Throw hands in the air.

Things to talk about:

1. What if Halloween lasted 12 days? Count to 12!
2. How would you celebrate Halloween for 12 days? Would you trick-or-treat every night. Would you have 12 costume parties? Would you bake twelve pumpkin pies?
3. If you gave a friend twelve spooky gifts, what would they be? Brainstorm! A tarantula? A bee wrapped in a box? A mushy banana?

Materials: None

Preparation: None

Things to do:

Sing the following song to the tune of *The 12 Days of Christmas*. Below are suggested body movements:

- Clap on the first line of each verse.
- On the second line of each verse, cross your arms over your chest for a love symbol!
- For a vampire bat - flap arms.
- For rats - make two fists, stick out your first fingers and wiggle them.
- For cats - use fingers to stroke whiskers.
- For brooms - place fingers together and move arms around.
- For spiders - stick out your first fingers and spin them around.
- For beetles - crawl with your fingers on the rug.
- For toads - make fists and hop them down your thighs.
- For monsters - mash palms together.
- For mummies - place arms straight out and move them up and down.
- For ghosts - spread out fingers on your hands and move them around.
- For worms - wiggle your fingers.
- For apples - throw fists in the air three times in a row!

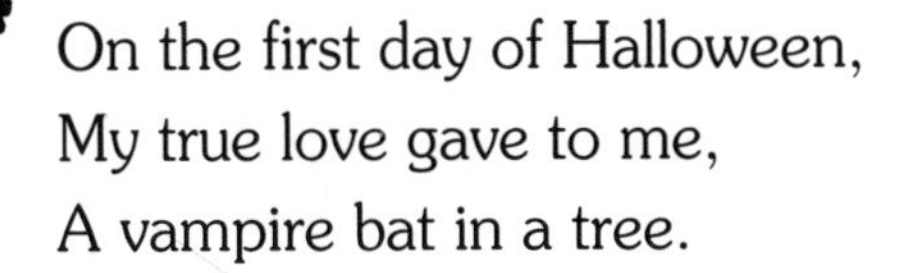

On the first day of Halloween,
My true love gave to me,
A vampire bat in a tree.

On the second day of Halloween,
My true love gave to me,
Two white rats,
And a vampire bat in a tree.

On the third day of Halloween,
My true love gave to me,
Three black cats,
Two white rats,
And a vampire bat in a tree.

On the fourth day of Halloween,
My true love gave to me,
Four brooms a-flying,
Three black cats,
Two white rats,
And a vampire bat in a tree.

On the fifth day of Halloween,
My true love gave to me,
Five spiders spinning,
Four brooms a-flying,
Three black cats,
Two white rats,
And a vampire bat in a tree.

On the sixth day of Halloween,
My true love gave to me,
Six beetles crawling,
Five spiders spinning,
Four brooms a-flying,
Three black cats,
Two white rats,
And a vampire bat in a tree.

On the seventh day of Halloween,
My true love gave to me,
Seven toads a-hopping,
Six beetles crawling,
Five spiders spinning,
Four brooms a-flying,
Three black cats,
Two white rats,
And a vampire bat in a tree.

On the eighth day of Halloween,
My true love gave to me,
Eight monsters mashing,
Seven toads a hopping,
Six spiders spinning,
Four brooms a-flying,
Three black cats,
Two white rats,
And a vampire bat in a tree.

On the ninth day of Halloween,
My true love gave to me,
Nine mummies moaning,
Eight monsters mashing,
Seven toads a-hopping,
Six beetles crawling,
Five spiders spinning,
Four brooms a-flying,
Three black cats,
Two white rats,
And a vampire bat in at tree.

On the tenth day of Halloween,
My true love gave to me,
Ten ghosts a-groaning,
Nine mummies moaning,
Eight monsters mashing,
Seven toads a-hopping,
Six beetles crawling,
Five spiders spinning,
Four brooms a-flying,
Three black cats,
Two white rats,
And a vampire bat in a tree.

On the eleventh day of Halloween,
My true love gave to me,
Eleven worms a-wiggling,
Ten ghosts a-groaning,
Nine mummies moaning,
Eight monsters mashing,
Seven toads a-hopping,
Six beetles crawling,
Five spiders spinning,
Four brooms a-flying,
Three black cats,
Two white rats,
And a vampire bat in a tree.

On the twelveth day of Halloween,
My true love gave to me,
Twelve rotten apples!
Eleven worms a-wiggling,
Ten ghosts a-groaning,
Nine mummies moaning,
Eight monsters mashing,
Seven toads a-hopping,
Six beetles crawling,
Five spiders spinning,
Four brooms a-flying,
Three black cats,
Two white rats,
And a vampire bat in a tree.

More Ideas:

- As you are learning the song, have the children say the last word in each line.

Think Like a Turkey!

Things to talk about:

1. Ask the question: "If a turkey walked into the classroom, what do you think it would look like?" Follow up with a picture of a turkey.
2. Why do you think people eat turkey at Thanksgiving? Brainstorm! Many years ago, when people started the tradition of having large feasts together, there were many wild turkeys in the area.
3. Instead of turkey, what else could you serve at Thanksgiving? Think of other types of meat or birds.

Materials:

Paper, a pen, scissors, a pot, a feather

Preparation:

Cut strips of paper. Print the suggested questions and multiple choice answers on the strips of paper. Place them in a pot.

Things to do:

1. Place the pot on the rug. Sit around the pot. Choose a child to stir the pot of turkey questions with the feather.
2. This child can then choose a paper strip. Read the question. The child can try to guess the answer from the choices offered.

3. Suggested questions and answers:
   - Is a male turkey one foot or two feet or three feet tall? (three feet)
   - Which color does a turkey NOT have on him? red? brown? green? purple? (purple)
   - Is a male turkey called a tom, a tim or a tootsie? (a tom)
   - There are spots on a turkey egg. Are they blue, red or yellow? (red)
   - There is a part, on a turkey, that has no feathers. Is it the turkey's stomach, neck or head? (Head!)
   - Does a turkey spend the night in a cave, in a tree, or on the ground? (in a tree)
   - Which is bigger - a chicken egg or a turkey egg? (a turkey egg)
   - Does a turkey have poor eyesight or good eyesight? (good eyesight)
   - When a turkey gets excited, does he faint, or pull out his feathers, or does his head change color. (His head changes color.)
   - When a turkey is frightened, does he make a sound like chug-chug-chug, or turc-turc-turc, or peep-peep-peep! (turc-turc-turc)
   - A turkey makes a noise that sounds like: gubble, gubble, gubble, or gump, gump, gump, or gobble, gobble, gobble? (gobble!)
   - Which type of food does a turkey NOT eat?—blueberries, snails, lizards or rabbits? (rabbits)
   - There is a fleshy red growth that hangs at the base of the beak. Is this called a boom, a mush or a snood? (a snood.)
   - There are fleshy bumps that grow down a turkey's neck. Are these called wiggles, wattles or wumps? (wattles)
   - Do wild turkeys live in woods, rainforests, or lakes? (woods)

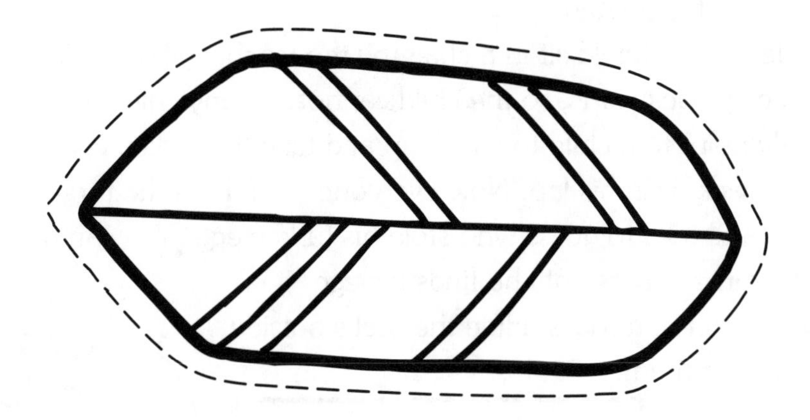

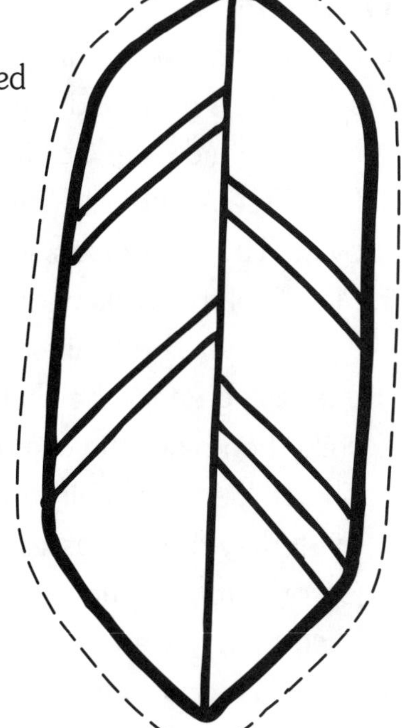

More Ideas:

- Stuff a turkey. Have everyone tear newspaper into strips. Stuff a large paper bag with the strips. Tie the top of the bag with red yarn. Reproduce and cut out a turkey head. Tape or staple the head on the bag. Reproduce and glue feathers all over the bag body.

Things to talk about:

1. If you were a turkey, what color would your feathers be? How big would you be? What would you do all day? Brainstorm!
2. Make up a turkey song. Have everyone help think of words and rhythms.
3. Make up a turkey game. What materials would you need? What would you call your game?
4. Make rhythms with the word turkey. Clap the word. Snap the word. Stomp your feet while you say turkey. What else can you do while you say turkey?

Materials:

A feather, turkey stickers and rocks, at least one for each child

Preparation:

Place the stickers on the rocks.

Things to do:

1. Play Duck, Duck, Turkey. As you walk around the circle, carry a turkey feather. When you tap someone's head and say turkey, give them the feather before they chase you.
2. Make up a dance. Call it the Turkey Trot.
3. Play Freeze Turkey. Play the Freeze dance song. If you are caught moving, sit down in the oven. The last person standing does not get eaten.
4. Play Fool the Turkey. Sit in a circle. Have a child sit in a chair, by the teacher. (This child is the turkey.) The chair should be facing backwards, so the child cannot see any children. Place a fake egg under the chair. Secretly point to a child to sneak up and take the turkey egg. This child then hides the egg behind his back or in his lap. Now everyone yells: Fool the turkey. The child in the chair turns around and tries to guess who stole his turkey egg. You can give the turkey three guesses, or let the turkey guess until he finds his egg.
5. Go on a turkey hunt. Place turkey stickers on rocks. Hide the rocks outside. Each rock represents a turkey. Hunt for them.
6. Sing this song to the tune of *Ring Around The Rosie*.

Ring around the turkey,
Pocket full of jerky,
Feathers, feathers,
We all gobble down!

More Ideas:

- Have some turkey jerky in your pocket. Share it.

Things to talk about:

1. What does it mean to follow directions? Brainstorm!
2. When is it important to follow directions? Answers might be: when you are following a recipe; when you are following a map; when you follow traffic signs; when you are learning to play a game.
3. Why is it important to follows directions in a classroom?
4. Ask the children to follow your movements. Suggested movements might be: shaking both hands in the air, rotating a foot, bending at the waist, nodding your head.

Materials:

Masking tape

Preparation:

Take masking tape and stick it to the carpet in one large circle.

Things to do:

1. Stand around the circle. Pretend you are a turkey. The circle is a large oven.
2. Give everyone directions to follow. The only time a direction is not followed is when you say: Jump in the circle. The children who jump inside the circle are cooked. They can sit in the oven until the game is over, or until all the children have been tricked into jumping in the oven.
3. Below are suggestions for directions.

- Walk around the circle.
- Tiptoe around the circle.
- Walk with one foot out and one foot inside the circle.
- Fly around the circle.
- Crawl around the circle.
- Walk sideways along the circle tape.
- Balance on the tape as you walk, with arms out to your side.
- Walk backwards around the circle.

4. Say the words, jump in the circle, at least after every two or three directions.

More Ideas:

- Send a long string of yarn home with each child. They can form a yarn oven at home and play with their family members.

Pumpkin Imagination

Things to talk about:

1. Who has heard the story of Cinderella? What did her fairy godmother turn the pumpkin into? A coach.
2. What can you do with your imagination? Anything. If you could turn a pumpkin into something else, what would it be? An orange treasure chest? A ball? A pumpkin pie?
3. If you woke up, and your head turned into a pumpkin, what would you do? Put a paper bag over your head? Paint your face on the pumpkin? Put a wig on the pumpkin?
4. What if everyone had a pumpkin for a head? What would the rest of your body look like?

Materials:

Butcher paper, tape, a pie pan, a black marker

Preparation:

Cut a long sheet of butcher paper. Tape it low on a wall.

Things to do:

1. Trace a pie pan, on the butcher paper, to make a circle shape. Trace as many pie pans as there are children.
2. Ask for volunteers to draw a face inside one of the circles. Give this child a black marker. Encourage the child to draw eyes, a nose, a mouth, ears, hair and even eyebrows.
3. When everyone has drawn a face, take the marker and draw a stem at the top of each face. What have you made? Pumpkin faces.
4. What is another name for a pumpkin face? A jack-o'-lantern
5. Print each child's name under their pumpkin. Print the letters so they follow the bottom curve of the pumpkin.

More Ideas:

- Draw pumpkin shapes on a second sheet of butcher paper. Provide markers. What else can you make the pumpkin shapes into?